Anonymous

Dinner to Señor Matias Romero

Anonymous

Dinner to Señor Matias Romero

ISBN/EAN: 9783744784658

Printed in Europe, USA, Canada, Australia, Japan

Cover: Foto ©ninafisch / pixelio.de

More available books at **www.hansebooks.com**

DINNER

to

Señor Matias Romero,

Envoy Extraordinary and Minister Pleni-
potentiary from Mexico,

ON THE 29th OF MARCH, 1864.

For freedom's battle, once begun
Bequeathed by bleeding sire to son,
Though baffled oft, is ever won.

New York, February, 1866

Mexican Legation, January 22, 1866.

Honorable James W. Beekman:

My Dear Sir—It has for some time been my intention to publish a fine English edition, in pamphlet form, of the proceedings of the dinner given to me as the representative of the Mexican Republic, on the 29th day of March, 1864, by distinguished citizens of your metropolis, to express their sympathy for the cause of Mexican independence and liberty.

My engagements and pressing public duties (which are much more onerous since our collision with France) have prevented hitherto the accomplishment of my object. Meanwhile, the lamented President Lincoln did us the honor to submit, officially, to the Senate of the United States, with his Message of June 16, 1864, covering correspondence on Mexican affairs, a translation of a Spanish account of that dinner, which original I had published some months previously for circulation in Mexico.

Although this official publication, in a great measure, answers my purpose, it has some typographical errors, and I think it would be well to republish those proceedings, adopting, however, as far as practicable, the text of the official documents.

It is only just that each of the gentlemen who then honored Mexico in my person be supplied with a copy of an authentic edition, as it is in my opinion a proof of their enlightened support of a sister Republic in her hour of utmost need, which elevates them as friends of mankind and citizens of a great Republic, called by its position to exercise untold influence on the destinies of man.

4

I venture, my dear friend, the trespass of confiding this edition to your care.

With renewed assurances of esteem,

I remain most truly yours,

M. ROMERO.

Mr. SEWARD TO Señor ROMERO.

DEPARTMENT OF STATE,　}
WASHINGTON, May 25, 1864. }

Mr. Seward presents his compliments to Señor Romero, and acknowledges, with sincere thanks, the receipt of the slip from the *New York Tribune*, of last Saturday, containing very much interesting information concerning affairs in Mexico, and the sentiment of friendly sympathy which is entertained by the national government toward the United States.

Señor M. ROMERO, &c., &c., &c.

Señor ROMERO TO Mr. SEWARD.

[TRANSLATION.]

[Private.] WASHINGTON, May 24, 1864.

ESTEEMED SIR—The *Herald*, of New York, of the 18th April last past, published an account of what occurred at a dinner which several distinguished persons of that city, friends of Mexico, had the kindness to give me on the 29th of March last. That portion of such account which relates to the remarks which I made, when called upon to speak by the persons who honored me with that demonstration, attributes to me some opinions which I never even thought of uttering, and is, in general, so little exact, that I think it proper to make known to you, although this can have only an indirect bearing on the official business of the department in your charge, that the inclosure herewith

contains a faithful narrative, written in Spanish, of all that passed at
that dinner, and an exact translation of what, on that occasion, I had
the honor to say in English.

I am, sir, very respectfully,

Your faithful servant,

M. ROMERO.

Hon. WILLIAM H. SEWARD, &c., &c., &c.

MR. SEWARD TO SEÑOR ROMERO.

WASHINGTON, May 25, 1864.

MY DEAR SIR—I beg to thank you for the authentic report, trans-
mitted with your note of the 24th instant, of the proceedings at the
banquet given to you by certain distinguished citizens of New York,
and which contains an exact translation of the remarks you made on
that occasion.

Although your note is unofficial, I shall place it with the printed
report on the files of the legation of Mexico in the Department of
State, to protect you from the misapprehensions which might result
from the incorrect published reports of your remarks to which you
allude.

I am, my dear sir, very truly yours,

WILLIAM H. SEWARD.

Señor MATIAS ROMERO, &c., &c., &c.

ON the evening of the 29th of March, 1864, a banquet
was given in this city, at Delmonico's Hotel, in the Fifth
Avenue, in honor of Señor Don MATIAS ROMERO, Minister
from Mexico, by citizens of New York, with the view of

B

manifesting their sympathy for that Republic in the present struggle against her French invaders.

About a month previously, some of our citizens projected a demonstration in favor of the Mexican cause, which, irrespective of Government policy, might elicit the dominant conviction in regard to that invasion.

The following invitation was therefore sent to Señor ROMERO:

NEW YORK, February 16, 1864.

DEAR SIR—The undersigned, in common with many loyal citizens, feel much interest in the present condition of Mexico, that important Continental State.

We cordially sympathize with the people of Mexico in their unequal struggle, and, appreciating their bravery and sacrifices, and your services in maintaining the integrity of your country, we tender to you, as the faithful representative of Mexico, a dinner in this city, on Tuesday, March 29th.

Your obedient servants,

WILLIAM C. BRYANT,	GEORGE T. STRONG,
WILLIAM H. ASPINWALL,	HENRY DELAFIELD,
HAMILTON FISH,	HENRY E. PIERREPONT,
JOHN W. HAMERSLEY,	GEORGE OPDYKE,
JONATHAN STURGES,	DAVID DUDLEY FIELD,
JAMES W. BEEKMAN,	GEORGE BANCROFT,
J. J. ASTOR, JR,	C. A. BRISTED,
SMITH CLIFT,	ALEXANDER VAN RENSSELAER,
W. E. DODGE, JR.,	GEORGE FOLSOM,
DAVID HOADLEY,	WASHINGTON HUNT,
FREDERICK DE PEYSTER,	CHARLES KING,
W. BUTLER DUNCAN,	WILLARD PARKER,
WILLIAM CURTIS NOYES,	ADRIAN ISELIN,
HENRY CLEWS,	ROBERT J. LIVINGSTON,
FREDERICK C. GEBHARD,	SAMUEL B. RUGGLES,

JAMES T. BRADY.

His Excellency M. ROMERO,
Mexican Minister, &c., &c., &c., Washington, D. C.

SEÑOR ROMERO'S ANSWER.

MEXICAN LEGATION IN THE UNITED STATES OF AMERICA,
WASHINGTON, March 20, 1864.

GENTLEMEN—I have just had the honor to receive your kind letter of the 18th ultimo, informing me that you, in common with many loyal citizens, feel much interest in the present condition of Mexico, cordially sympathize with the people of that republic in their unequal struggle, and appreciating their bravery and sacrifices, as well as my services (you kindly add) in maintaining the integrity of my country, you are good enough to tender to me, as the representative of Mexico, a dinner in your city on the 29th instant.

Nothing could be more gratifying to myself and to my countrymen than seeing that we have with us the enlightened and uninterested sympathy of so many of the most distinguished and eminent citizens, whose virtues, learning, and persevering enterprise have made of the city of New York the great metropolis of the New World.

The demonstration with which you intend to honor the noble cause for which my country is fighting against one of the strongest and best organized military powers on earth, while it shows your high opinion of the question, and your great sense of justice, will be duly appreciated and thanked for by my Government and countrymen, as well as by all unbiased and disinterested people throughout the world, who have some regard for justice, and can not help noticing it entirely trampled down by the Emperor of the French in the policy he is pursuing toward Mexico.

I am, gentlemen, very respectfully,

Your obedient servant,

M. ROMERO.

Messrs. WILLIAM CULLEN BRYANT, &c., &c., and all the other gentlemen who signed this invitation.

THE feast was held in four of the largest saloons at Delmonico's. Two were set apart for the reception and convenience of the guests, the third for the banquet, and the fourth for the orchestra.

The great dining hall was illuminated as a promenade for the families of the hosts and guests, and a large concourse of ladies and gentlemen, who were invited to see the table and be presented to the distinguished Envoy.

Tasteful and appropriate additions had been made to the furniture and decorations of those princely apartments.

Exquisite flowers, native and exotic, were grouped with artistic skill and classic elegance; here festooned from arch to arch, there pendent from the fretted ceilings, or, with tropical luxuriance, gracefully bent from massive vases.

Doorways, étagères, all arrayed in fragrant wreaths and garlands, were eloquent with expressions of sympathy that need no interpreter but cultivated taste. Opposite mirrors repeated the gorgeous scene.

At the head of the banquet-hall were the flags of the two nations; on the table five vast bouquets of various shapes flanked a "pièce montée" that Carême might envy, blazoning the arms of Mexico; the eagle erect on the cactus, growing on a rock, which seems to rise from mid-ocean.

The honor of

company

is requested at a **DINNER**, in compliment to

Señor Romero,

Envoy Extraordinary and Minister Plenipotentiary from Mexico,

at Delmonico's 5th Avenue on Tuesday March 29th at 7 o'clock.

New York,

March 21st 1864.

Stewards.
- John Jacob Astor.
- Henry Clews
- John W. Shinnersly.

The palm and the cactus, types of the flora of Mexico, stood at either end. On pyramids of sugar were inscribed the names of Juarez, and other statesmen of Mexico. At each cover was a card, with appropriate name, surmounted by the Mexican arms, engraved in gold. The *menu* was blue satin in gold letters.

The saloon and table presented a *coup d'œil* seldom paralleled in any country or at any period.

Helmsmuller, long a resident of Mexico, and familiar with her sweet and striking airs, by skillful adaptation introduced *La Jaroba* and *La Sinolita* into a spirited march ; and, in concerted order, the Chairman led the guest of the night to the honored seat. Señor Romero seemed much gratified that the cadences of the *Tertulia* should greet him on the Atlantic slope.

Señor Don Juan N. Navarro, Consul-General of the Mexican Republic, resident at New York, Señor Don Ignacio Mariscal, an eminent jurist of Mexico, now Secretary of the Mexican Legation in the United States, and Don Fernando de la Cuesta, Assistant Secretary of the Legation, were invited guests.

ORDER AT TABLE.

Mr. BEEKMAN,

Señor ROMERO,	Mr. ISELIN,
Mr. BRYANT,	Mr. GEBHARD,
Mr. DELAFIELD,	Mr. HAMERSLEY,
Mr. DUNCAN,	Mr. CLEWS,
Mr. ASTOR,	Mr. HUNT,
Señor CUESTA,	Mr. BANCROFT,
Mr. DE PEYSTER,	Mr. STURGES,
Mr. PIERREPONT,	Mr. FOLSOM,
Mr. CLIFT,	Mr. BRISTED,
Dr. NAVARRO,	Mr. DODGE,
Dr. PARKER,	Mr. FIELD,
Mr. OPDYKE,	Señor MARISCAL,

Mr. KING.

At nine o'clock the Chairman called the company to order.

Mr. BEEKMAN.

Gentlemen—We are met to do honor to the great cause of religious and political freedom, now contended for, against fearful odds, by our neighbor, the Republic of Mexico.

In welcoming her Minister and Representative, we mean to show our good-will toward his country.

Our hearts are so full, we have so much to say, that I venture upon a Mexican pronunciamiento, and interrupt your feast midway, by a revolutionary innovation, while I give, as the first regular toast—

The President of the United States. (Enthusiastic cheers—the company rising.)

I call on Mr. David Dudley Field to reply.

Mr. DAVID DUDLEY FIELD.

Mr. Chairman—Why I should be called upon to answer this toast, I do not precisely know. I hold, as you, sir, are aware, no official position, and am in no manner entitled to speak, except as any citizen may, for the President or any member of his cabinet. So far as the toast is a compliment or salutation for the country of which he is the first magistrate, we who are Americans all share, both in giving and receiving it. So far as it calls for the expression of any opinion or intention on the part of the Executive, I, of course, can say nothing.

There is one respect, however, in which all of us, private citizens, may venture to speak for the Chief Magistrate, and that is when we interpret or express the judgment of the American people. Here, more than anywhere else, the executive department of the government is the agent and exponent of the popular will. The President may, it is true, have information not immediately accessible to the public, and, acting upon it, may decide in a manner which the public does not at first approve; but, in the end, when the information becomes general, the conclusions at which the nation arrives give law to cabinets and presidents.

When, therefore, we utter the opinion of the American people, we answer, in a great measure, for the President; and in this manner any private citizen, like myself, may venture to speak. So doing, I assert, without hesitation, that, with unexampled unanimity, Americans feel a profound sympathy for the Mexican people in this day of their trial. The sentiment of the country is all but one on this subject. We do not stop to inquire whether the Mexicans have not made mistakes in the management of their affairs. That is possible; all nations have done as much. We have done so in the management of our own affairs, of which we are now reaping the bitter fruits. But, whatever may have been the mistakes of the Mexicans, they give no sort of excuse for the invasion of the French, or the attempt of foreigners to impose a yoke upon their country.

This invasion we regard as one of the greatest crimes of our age. To war with a neighboring nation, whose proximity naturally gives rise to irritating questions, is a great evil; but to carry fire and sword among a distant and unoffending people, is a barbarous and cruel wrong, which shocks the conscience of the world, and which history will execrate as it execrates the partition of Poland.

Though the minds and hearts of the American people are chiefly occupied with their own long and bloody struggle against an unnatural rebellion, they nevertheless feel deeply the wrongs of Mexico, and they will express this feeling on every proper occasion. We express it here at this festive gathering; they will express it at public meetings, in State Legislatures, and in Congress; and they expect the Executive, the organ of the nation, in its intercourse with other nations, to express it also to the fullest extent, within the limits of international obligations.

Not only do we give the Mexican people our sincerest sympathy, but we offer them all the encouragement which a neutral nation can offer. We bid them to be of good cheer; to hold fast by their integrity; to stand firm through all vicissitudes, believing in the strength of nationality, in the vitality of freedom, and in that overruling and all-wise Providence which, sooner or later, chastises wrong and casts down the oppressor.

This is not the place to enter upon a discussion of the motives which prompted this French invasion, nor to trace the history of the parties which have divided Mexico, and been made the pretext for the intrusion of foreigners into its domestic affairs. Thus much, however, may be said, that whatever may be the incidental questions that have arisen, there is one great and controlling feature in the controversy: and that is the claim, on the one hand, of the Church to interfere in the affairs of the State; and the claim of the State, on the other hand, to be freed from the interference of the Church. We hear constantly of the Church party in Mexico. Why should there be a Church party? What can it have legitimately to do with secular affairs? With us it has been a fundamental maxim, from the formation of our Government, imbedded in the organic law, that there must be forever a total separation of Church and State. The Mexican people—that is to say, the true and loyal portion of them—are struggling for the same end; and in this we Americans, of all creeds and all parties, bid them

God speed. Yes, all of us, excepting only the rebel, who raises his arms against his country, and the deceitful renegade, who, not daring to raise an arm against it, seeks yet to betray it: all of us, I say, with these exceptions, pray for and believe in the deliverance of Mexico. It may be sooner or later; it may come through greater misfortunes than any which she has yet suffered, but come it will. The spirit of freedom is stronger than the lances of France.

Maximilian may come with the Austrian eagle and the French tricolor; he may come with a hundred ships; he may march on the high road from Vera Cruz to the capital, under the escort of French squadrons; he may be proclaimed by French trumpets in all the squares of the chief cities; but he will return, at some earlier or later day, a fugitive from the New World back to the Old, from which he came; his followers will be scattered and chased from the land; the titles and dignities which he is about to lavish on parasites and apostates will be marks of derision; the flag of the republic will wave from all the peaks of the Cordilleras, and be answered from every mountain-top, east and west, to either ocean; and the renewed country, purified by blood and fire, will resume its institutions, and be free.

Such, Mr. Chairman, are, I am sure, the wishes and the expectations of the American people; and this, I am bound to presume, would be the answer, if he were free to speak, of the President of the United States.

The dinner was resumed. When the dessert was served, the Chairman gave the second regular toast—

Don Benito Juarez—Constitutional President of the Mexican Republic. (Great enthusiasm.)

This illustrious man is of pure indigenous race. Of humble birth his eminent virtues raised him to the chief magistracy of his country, and, under the most adverse circumstances, he has always ably and irreproachably discharged his difficult duties.

c

May we ask the honored President of Columbia College to speak to us of JUAREZ?

MR. KING.

GENTLEMEN—The toast you have just drunk to the President of the Mexican republic is worthy of our cheers, for he is the chosen representative of the Mexican people, from whom he himself sprang, and our distinguished guest to-day is accredited to our Government as the representative of the Government of which President Juarez is the head. In honoring the name of President Juarez, we are, then, acting in harmony with the views and policy of our own Government as much as in consonance with our own feelings and convictions.

For certainly to us, as Americans, there is much in the character and antecedents of Juarez to commend him to our regard. He is, what was the boast of the Athenians of old (that noblest race of men that ever made a small state great), born of the soil, and of the people, where he lives—one of those autochthones who, having no progenitors to look back to but mother earth, have all the more inducement to look forward to ennobling, as far as they may, and dignifying, that mother earth.

Thoroughly trained and educated in all good knowledge, Juarez labors to see his country great, prosperous, and, above all, *free*—free individually and socially—free politically, and, above all, spiritually free. It is there that lies the danger and the difficulty of Mexico. It is spiritual bondage even more than partisan and factious quarrels that has damaged that fine country. It is the influence of a class of religionists as a power in the state that has been most injurious there, as it must be everywhere; and I say this in the most general terms, and not as applicable to any one form of belief.

Juarez is the avowed and bold opponent of the politico-religious hierarchy which has so largely controlled the affairs of Mexico, while monopolizing a most undue share of its wealth.

He is proscribed by the priesthood, because he stands, as in New

England our forefathers did, for liberty of conscience, for the right of every man to decide for himself in matters of faith. For the same reason he is proscribed by the imperial pro-consul of France; for it suits the present interest of the unfathomable mystery that sits upon the throne of France to cultivate the Roman Catholic hierarchy, which is a united body all over the world, wielding a sword—and that not the sword of the Spirit—of which "the hilt is at Rome, and the point everywhere."

We, who have tried and known how much safer and wiser it is to separate the Church from the State—and where public opinion, and sometimes positive law, forbids the mingling of priests in politics—we can well sympathize with President Juarez in his brave struggle in Mexico against a domineering clergy and against the foreign allies whom they have introduced into the country, to ruin where they could no longer rule.

In the midst of the agony of our own civil war, we can not be insensible nor indifferent to the cause of Mexico, our neighbor, our friend, our natural ally in every difficulty that shall involve the point of American nationality and American interests, as opposed to European nationality and European interests. Mexico never can, with the assent of the people of the United States, become the appendage of a European nation, or furnish a peaceful throne to any scion of a European imperial house. The opportunity, so auspiciously presented by the visit of our distinguished guest, is eagerly embraced by us—private individuals, indeed, yet not unfair representatives of the popular sentiments of our fellow-citizens of all classes—to give emphatic expression to the declaration that, "biding our time," we will, at all hazards, when that time comes, assert and uphold the doctrine that on this continent we will not permit the interference by arms of any European nation to overthrow republican institutions and to establish monarchy. Especially as respects Mexico (conterminous with us for so many degrees of longitude, washed on its Atlantic and Pacific shores by the same bays and seas, and anxious to model its institutions after those which have raised these United States to such power and prosperity), with respect to Mexico, I repeat, we can not, and we will not, consent that any archduke of Austria, be he puppet or be he principal, nor any other monarchical pretender, shall be imposed upon the Mexican people by foreign bayonets.

True, it is, alas! that, through the great crimes of slavery, we are at this moment unable to give to our firm purposes in this regard fitting outward manifestation; but, as in the inevitable course of justice, which is God, our civil war must ere long close by the extirpation of its accursed cause, and in the restoration of our national unity and territorial integrity, we shall then have disposable such a force on sea and on land as will impart unlimited power of persuasion to the diplomatic declaration we shall then make, that Mexico must and shall be Mexican; that Mexico must and shall be American, and not European. (Cheers.)

The CHAIRMAN.

We are now to listen to our guest, the representative of Mexico.

Señor ROMERO.

Mr. Chairman—Gentlemen—I feel entirely unable to express to you in a sufficient manner my sincere thanks for the great honor you have bestowed upon me and my country in this refined and splendid demonstration of your sympathy for struggling Mexico. It is, indeed, particularly gratifying to me that this significant demonstration is made by so many of the most distinguished and most eminent citizens, who are an ornament to this great metropolis, and whose virtues, learning, and enterprise have contributed so much to make your city in so brief a period the first, not only of the broad United States, but of the whole American continent, as well as to make your country one of the most powerful, wealthy, and civilized on the globe.

It is, indeed, another motive which greatly adds to my gratification, and for which, in the name of my country, I beg to express to you my gratitude for the kind words with which our distinguished friend has proposed the health of Benito Juarez, the constitutional President of the republic of Mexico, and for the prompt heartiness and cordiality with which that toast has been received. I perceive, with joy and gratitude, gentlemen, that you appreciate the high qualities of that statesman and patriot, and hold a strong and pure sympathy for the noble cause of which he is the leader.

I am rejoiced that I have the opportunity to see with my own eyes the proof that the eminent French statesman, M. Thiers, was somewhat mistaken when, in a speech he recently delivered before the Corps Législatif, of Paris, against the policy pursued by the Emperor Napoleon in Mexican affairs, he stated that the United States would not, under present circumstances, object in any way to that policy; and that, should the Archduke Maximilian come to this city *en route* to Mexico, he would meet with a cordial reception at your hands. It could scarcely be possible to have a more distinguished, complete, and genuine representation of the patriotism, intelligence, and wealth of the great city of New York—the leading city of the Union—than that I see assembled here this evening; yet, if I can trust my senses, gentlemen, I venture to assert that the sympathies of your great city run in a direction very different from that imagined by M. Thiers.

I am very happy to say that the kind feeling you express for Mexico is fully reciprocated. In Mexico there are now but the sentiments of regard and admiration for the United States, and the desire to pursue such a course as will draw more closely all those powerful ties by which both nations should be united.

It has sometimes appeared to me, that the gentlemen who controlled the Government of the United States for thirty-five years previous to 1861, cared for nothing so much as for the acquisition of territory. Those gentlemen thus caused their country to appear in the character of a very covetous man, who, without knowing the boundaries of his own estate, or endeavoring to improve it, constantly exerts himself to enlarge its limits, without being very scrupulous as to the means of its accomplishment.

Just before the war with Mexico commenced, the United States had a boundary question with England, which threatened a rupture between the two countries, and I have been informed that the same documents which were prepared as a declaration of war against Great Britain were used when war was finally declared against Mexico. Thus, while the idea of acquiring domain from Great Britain by a dubious title, to say the least, was relinquished, the same scheme was carried out against Mexico, not only without any plausible reason, but, I must say, in violation of all principles of justice.

I beg of you, gentlemen, to excuse me if I have referred to an unpleasant point in the history of late events. But I wish to forcibly present to your minds the idea that the unfair policy I have alluded to led, in a great measure, to the troubles and complications in which you are now involved, and one of the consequences of which is French intervention in Mexico, as that intervention would never have been but for the civil war in the United States.

Those who have pursued this policy appear to have been, in the main, under the influence of the slave power, and to have had in view their own political influence and personal aggrandizement, rather than the great interests of their country. They very properly thought that, by extending the area of slavery, they would extend in proportion their influence and strength. For that reason they did not insist on increasing the territory of the United States in the far northwest, where their *peculiar institution* could not be acclimated, but rather set their eyes toward the sunny regions of Mexico. By that means the institution of human slavery had so large an increase, that a short time afterward it was strong enough to commence a gigantic war against the Government of the United States. In my opinion, the leaders of the slavery party always had in view the separation of their own States from the free States of the North, and to replace the loss of Northern aimed at the acquisition of Southern territory.

I will not conceal from you, gentlemen, the fact that we have looked with deep apprehension upon such an aggressive policy, which threatened to deprive us of our independence and nationality—the highest and most precious rights that man can enjoy on earth. We

were, of course, fully determined not to give up this precious inheritance, and we had resolved to fight to the last. In our present war
with France, we are giving a proof of our determination. It may
appear foolish and unavailing for Mexico, that has been so often ex-
hausted in her struggles to obtain true liberty during the last forty
years, to accept war with the greatest military power in Europe; but
there are circumstances in the life of nations which cause them to
overlook all secondary considerations, and determine to exert themselves to overcome all difficulties. Besides, our situation is not so
bad as many think.

Fortunately, the change of policy toward Mexico operated in the
United States brought up a consequent change in the feelings of my
country in regard to yours. We do not wish now to have any interest
antagonistical to yours, because we mean to keep peace with you, and
that object could scarcely be accomplished if our respective interests
were in opposition. For that reason, among other very material ones
that we had, we established a republican form of government and
democratic institutions, modeled on the same basis as yours.

The Emperor of the French pretends that the object of his interference in Mexican affairs is to prevent the annexation of Mexico to
the United States; and yet that very result would, most likely, be
ultimately accomplished if a monarchy were established in Mexico.
Fortunately for us, that scheme is by no means a feasible one.

Mexico is most bountifully blessed by Nature. She can produce
of the best quality and in large quantities all of the principal agricul-
tural staples of the world—cotton, coffee, sugar, tobacco, vanilla, wheat,
and corn. Her mines have yielded the largest portion of all the silver
which now circulates throughout the world, and there still remain to
her mountains of that precious metal, as well as of gold, which only
require labor, skill, and capital to make them available and valuable.
The wealth of California is nothing when compared with what still
remains in Mexico.

My country, therefore, opens a most desirable field for the enterprise of a commercial nation. Far-sighted England discovered this

many years ago, and by establishing a line of mail steamers from Southampton to Vera Cruz and Tampico, and negotiating advantageous treaties of commerce, has, beyond all other nations, enjoyed the best of the Mexican trade. France, seeing this, and wishing to vie with England, has undertaken an enterprise which, besides being ruinous to her, will not produce the desired end, as the means adopted must surely cause the opposite result. The United States are the best situated to avail of the immense wealth of Mexico. Being a neighbor nation, they have more advantages than any other for the frontier and coasting trade; and, furthermore, being a nation second to none in wealth, activity, skill, and enterprise, they are called by nature to speculate and enjoy the resources of Mexico.

We are willing to grant to the United States every commercial facility that will not be derogatory of our independence and sovereignty. This will give to the United States all possible advantages that could be derived from annexation, without any of its inconveniences. That once done, our common interests, political as well as commercial, will give us a common whole American continental policy which no European nation would dare disregard.

The bright future which I plainly see for both nations had made me forget for a moment the present troubles in which they are now involved. I consider these troubles of so transitory a nature as not to interfere materially with the common destiny I have foreshadowed; but, as they have the interest of actuality, I beg to be allowed to make a few remarks in regard to them.

Every careful observer of events could not help noticing, when the expedition against Mexico was organized in Europe, that it would, sooner or later, draw the United States into the most serious complications, and involve them in the difficulty. The object of that expedition being no less than a direct and armed interference in the political affairs of an American nation, with a view to overthrow its republican institutions and establish on their ruins a monarchy, with a European prince on the throne,—the only question to be determined by the United States and the other nations concerned, was as to the

21

time when they would be willing or ready to meet the issue thus
boldly and openly held out by the antagonistic nations of Europe.

The United States could not be indifferent in this question; just
as a man who sees his neighbor's house set on fire by an incendiary,
could not remain an unconcerned spectator, while his own house contains his family and all his fortune, and combustible matter lies in the
basement. The only alternative left to him should be, whether it
would be more convenient to his interests to help his neighbor in
putting out the fire from the beginning, and with the same earnest-
ness as if his own house were already caught by that destructive ele-
ment, or to wait inactive until the incendiary has succeeded in making
a perfect blaze of his neighbor's property, by which all will inevitably
be involved in one common ruin.

This, in my opinion, is the situation in which the United States
are placed with regard to Mexico. Taking into consideration the
well-known sagacity of American statesmen, the often-proved devotion
of the American people to republican institutions, and the patriotism
and zeal of the Administration that presides over the destinies of the
country, I can not entertain the slightest doubt that the United States
will act in this emergency as will conduce to the best interests they
and mankind at large have at stake in the Mexican question.

In the mean time, however, I consider it of the highest importance
that the delusion prevailing throughout Europe that the United States
do not oppose, and rather favor, the establishment of a monarchy in
Mexico by French bayonets, should be dispelled. The French Government has been working steadily in causing that delusion to prevail
on the other side of the water, and, so far, has succeeded more than
could be expected, considering the absurdity of such an idea. The
war against Mexico would be ten times more unpopular in France
than it is now—in fact, it could not be maintained any longer—if the
French people were made to understand that the people of the United
States will never tolerate, much less favor or encourage, the establishment, by force of arms, of a European monarchy upon the ruins
of a sister neighboring republic. The French people are friendly to

D

the United States; old traditions, the common love of liberty, and the absence of opposing interests, make them friendly. They would, therefore, be wholly opposed to any thing that, without bringing them any real benefit, might, sooner or later, lead to a war with this country. They very well know that such a war could not but be disastrous to France, since France would have every thing to lose and nothing to gain by such a war, whatever may be her influence and power in the European continental politics.

The United States may find that they are brought squarely to the issue on the Mexican question sooner than they expected, should the report, lately reached here, of any understanding between Maximilian, as so-called emperor of Mexico, and the insurgents in this country, prove correct. The archduke, it is stated, will inaugurate his administration by acknowledging the independence of the South, and, perhaps, he will go further; and this, of course, by the advice, consent, and support of the French Government, whose satellite, and nothing else, will the archduke be in Mexico.

The French official and semi-official papers assure us that Maximilian will soon depart for Mexico. All present appearances indicate that he is willing to change his high position in Europe for a hazardous one in Mexico. He can not stay there unless supported by a French army, and he will not, therefore, be any thing more than the shadow of the French emperor. Should he ever have a different view or desire from the French Government, or even the French general-in-chief, he will be obliged to submit to the humiliating condition of forbearing to do that which he thinks best in a country where he will call himself emperor. As far as the personality of the Austrian duke is concerned, he is nothing. If he goes to Mexico to meddle in our affairs, we shall consider him as our enemy, and deal with him accordingly. We hold that in the political question which is being agitated in Mexico the person of the Austrian duke is not of much account; and whether he does or does not go there, that question can ultimately have only one possible solution—namely, the triumph and maintenance of republican institutions.

As far as I am concerned, I prefer that Maximilian should go to Mexico, so as to give the European dreamers on monarchies a fair chance to realize their dreams of America. As for Mexico, I can say that nothing that has transpired in my country should surprise any one who is familiar with our affairs. It is true that we have been unfortunate during the past year; we have lost nearly all the battles we have fought with the French; they have occupied some of our principal cities; they have blockaded our ports; but all these gains on the part of the French are nothing when compared with the elements of opposition and endurance which remain with the national Government of Mexico, ruling a people numbering eight millions, determinedly opposed to intervention, ready to fight, and fighting already for their independence; a country that will require half a million of soldiers to subdue and possess; naturally strong in defences, possessing inaccessible mountains, impracticable roads, where the patriots will be able to make a perpetual warfare upon the invader, until he is persuaded of the impossibility of accomplishing the conquest, or be compelled to leave for other causes. Such is the prospect before us, and that in case we could do nothing more than make a passive resistance. But we can do better than this.

Among the many events calculated to terminate immediately French intervention in Mexico, the European complications which threaten to cause a general war on that continent should be particularly mentioned. It is certainly wonderful that while Europe is in so insecure and agitated a condition, menaced by revolutions everywhere, and wrestling to recover its own existence and independence, the French emperor should be thinking about arranging other people's affairs, as if his own did not require his immediate and most particular attention.

The only serious support the French intervention had among the Mexicans was that afforded by the Church party, which was, in fact, the promoter and supporter of the intervention. The generals of the Church party have, with the aid of the French army, been conscripting Mexican citizens to make them fight with the foreign invader against their brothers and the independence of their country. The Church party expected, of course, as a small compensation for the services rendered to the intervention, that as soon as the French should take the city of Mexico they would restore the Church property confiscated by the National Government, and the *fueros* of the clergy, of which they had been deprived. But the French have thus far failed to do this. They discovered that the Church party was the weakest, and that with that party they had no chance of subduing the country. The French now wish to conciliate the liberal party by sustaining and enforcing all the important measures and laws decreed by the National Government. But the liberals of Mexico are true patriots, not partisans, and will not be conciliated so long as the foot of the invader is on Mexican soil. The policy of the French so incensed the Church party that they broke altogether with the French. The Archbishop of Mexico, who was a member of the so-called regency, withdrew at once, and was afterward dismissed by General Bazaine. The so-called supreme tribunal protested against those measures, and shared the fate of the archbishop. All the archbishops and bishops in the republic then joined in signing a protest, in which they declared the condition of the Church to be far worse than it ever was under the rule of the liberal government; that now they are not allowed even to issue their pastorals, a right never denied to them while the liberals were in power in the city of Mexico. The protest concluded by excommunicating the French Government, the French army in Mexico, all Mexicans who take sides with the French, and everybody who supports the French cause in any way. These proceedings have left the French without the support of the only part of the native population they ever had in their favor, and have combined against them all the elements of the country.

I fear that I have already imposed too much upon your kindness, and, in concluding my remarks, I beg to express my earnest and sincere desire that this demonstration may be the beginning of a new era of perpetual peace and cordiality in the relations between the United States and Mexico. (Prolonged cheers.)

The Chair.

There has been a belief, in some quarters, that no statesmen, worthy of the name, have arisen in Mexico—Guatimotzin, Hidalgo, Morelos, Ocampo, Lerdo, and Degollado, are names venerated in that country. I propose, then, that we honor the Statesmen of Mexico, and I call on Mr. Bancroft, who so well appreciates their fame, to reply.

Mr. Bancroft.

GENTLEMEN—Although I am not prepared to deliver an address worthy of this auditory, I can not refrain from replying and expressing my sentiments, as I have been called to reply to the toast which our president has just proposed to the statesmen of our neighboring sister republic. The struggle which for many long years the Mexican people have sustained against their interior tyrants has been an heroic struggle, worthy of a civilized and cultivated people, and in which the sympathies of the whole civilized world—of all the friends of political and religious liberty—ought to have been manifested in a frank and decided manner in behalf of the Mexican people, directed by the liberal party. I believe, gentlemen, that the cause of civil wars, not only in Mexico, but throughout all Spanish America, has been the clergy alone, who, when they come to acquire power in the State, always strive to overturn the government and to subordinate the temporal interests of society to their own. This attribute seems to belong principally to the Catholic clergy.

The struggle, then, in which up to this time the patriotic Mexicans have been engaged, was a holy struggle, and the sympathy of the whole people of the United States was with them—a people who, whatever may be their religious creeds, adopts as a fundamental principle the most complete religious liberty, and the absolute independence of the Church from the State.

But now the sympathy of the United States is increased for the Mexican people, when, in addition to the facts already mentioned, we find this people struggling for their independence and nationality against a European nation, which, taking advantage of the civil strife in which we were engaged, has sought to establish before our eyes a form of government in open antagonism to our own. We can not do less than receive this project in the same way as Europe would receive it were we to foment revolutions and establish republics on that continent.

Thus it is that those statesmen in the United States who aid us to emerge from our present difficulties, and to restore our power and legitimate influence, and those who in Mexico not only consummate the great work of establishing religious liberty on a solid basis, but who succeed in driving from their country the foreign invader, or at least keep the sacred fire of patriotism and of resistance to the invader burning, while we disembarrass ourselves of our complications, deserve, in the highest degree, our sincere and ardent homage.

Gentlemen, the Egyptians used to place a burning lamp at the feet of their royal corpses. On descending to the deep vaults in which the corpses were deposited, the lamp was naturally extinguished.

Let Europe place at Maximilian's feet the weak lamp of monarchical power. It will not burn in the free atmosphere of our continent.

THE CHAIR.

Mexico has illustrious poets, too, whose names, celebrated at home, we are glad to remember here—names such as Atarcon, Heredia, Gorosteza, Carpio, Calderon. Will Mr. Bryant, whom *we* delight to honor, do us the favor to speak for the poets? (Cheers.)

MR. BRYANT.

We of the United States have constituted ourselves a sort of police of this New World. Again and again have we warned off the highwaymen and burglars of the Old World who stand at the head of its governments, styling themselves conquerors. We have said to them, that if they attempted to pursue their infamous profession here they did it at their peril. But now, when this police is engaged in a deadly conflict with a band of ruffians, comes this Frenchman, knocks down an unoffending bystander, takes his watch and purse, strips him of his clothing, and makes off with the booty. This act of the French monarch is as base, cowardly, and unmanly as it is criminal and cruel. There is no person, acquainted, even in the slightest degree, with the political history of the times, who does not know that it would never have been perpetrated had not the United States been engaged in an expensive and bloody war within their own borders.

There is a proverbial phrase used by lawyers, who say of a purchaser of land who does not obtain a clear and undisputed title, that he has bought a lawsuit—paid out his money for a controversy in the courts. We may say of this Maximilian of Austria, that, in accepting the crown of Mexico from the hands of Napoleon, he has accepted, not an empire, but a quarrel—a present quarrel with the people of Mexico, and a prospective quarrel with the people of the United States. The rule of a branch of the Austrian family will be no less hateful to the Mexicans than that of the Austrian monarch is to the inhabitants of Venice. Its yoke will be hated because it is a foreign yoke, laid upon their necks by strangers; it will be hated because it is imposed by violence; it will be hated because that violence was accompanied by fraud; for never was there a more shallow and transparent deception than that of the convocation of notables, from whom Napoleon pretended to receive the supreme dominion over Mexico.

Then, as to the relations of this new emperor with the United States, does any one suppose that they can possibly be amicable? Does any one suppose that after our civil war is ended, as it soon will be, the numerous class whom it has trained to adventure, and made fond of a military life, will all remain quietly at home when the cause of liberty and independence in Mexico demands their aid? Does any man doubt that, whatever may be the course taken by our Government, they will cross the Mexican frontier by thousands, to take part in favor of the people of that country? The party of liberty in Mexico will then have its auxiliaries close at hand, in a contiguous region, while the succors which the despot will need to protect his usurped dominion will be far away beyond the Atlantic.

Yet I wonder not that Maximilian should covet the possession of so noble a principality as Mexico, provided he were allowed to govern it in peace. I remember that, a few years since, in making a voyage to Europe in one of our steamers, there was a passenger on board to whom we gave the name of the Knight of the " Woeful Countenance." He was a thin, dark man, dressed in black, with a very broad-brimmed hat, long features, and a most sorrowful aspect. I learned that he was a Mexican, and entered into conversation with him. He described the natural advantages and resources of his country with much of that eloquence which I believe is the natural inheritance of the Latin race. He spoke of its mountains, pregnant with ores of the precious and useful metals; its vast plains and valleys of exhaustless fertility; its variety of climates—in some regions possessing the temperature of perpetual spring, in which were reared all the productions of the temperate zone, and in the other places basking under a torrid sun, which ripens all the fruits of the tropics to their most perfect maturity. Yet these rich mines were unwrought, these fertile fields untilled, these regions, with the climate of Paradise, thinly peopled by a race without enterprise, nearly without arts, and living almost from hand to mouth. This unhappy state of the country he attributed to the want of a permanent, enlightened, and liberal government, which, while maintaining peace and order, and securing to every man his individual rights as a freeman, left open every path of lawful enterprise.

We thought that we saw the dawn of this era of enlightened government in the administration of Juarez. That dawn has been overcast by the clouds of a tempest wafted hither from Europe. May the darkness which has gathered over it be of short continuance; may these clouds be soon dispelled by the sunshine of liberty and peace, and Mexico, assured in her independence, take the high place which belongs to her in the family of nations. (Continued applause.)

The Chair.

We have among our guests a distinguished lawyer of Mexico, Señor Don Ignacio Mariscal, Secretary of the Legation. I propose,

Our guest and the Bar of Mexico, which he adorns.

Señor MARISCAL.

Gentlemen—I never was more sorry than now for not having the control of your expressive language, that I might give a full utterance to my sentiments. Yet I can not help saying a few words to thank you very warmly for the kind and splendid manner in which you are complimenting the representative of my country, as well as for the enthusiastic allusions you have made and applauded in honor of its leading patriots and distinguished men. Finally, gentlemen, the toast you have just dedicated to me, and the too benevolent terms in which it was proposed, are things which I am not able to be thankful for in a sufficient way. I am perfectly aware that the general feeling of the people of the United States is most favorable to Mexico in her present struggle to resist conquest. But when I see that feeling shared by such prominent and enlightened citizens as you are, gentlemen, I consider it is not a blind sentiment, but rather a conviction, a deep sense of right and justice, as well as the knowledge of a danger common to both republics. I cherish the idea that while this unanimous sympathy for Mexico exists, my country will not be subjugated for a long time by the brutal force of a European army. The day will soon come, I trust, in which the sympathies of this great people will be no longer disregarded by any power in the world. You know, better than I do, which are the clouds now darkening your political horizon and preventing the break of that promising day. May they be soon dispelled! The sun of America will then shine triumphant upon the end of your national disturbances and the direful sufferings of Mexico. (Cheers.)

E

The Chair.

The President, the statesmen, the poets, and the bar of Mexico have been duly toasted—shall we forget her diplomacy? Our guest to-night is himself one of his country's ablest representatives. Yet I ask you to join me in complimenting another—a name well-known in Europe, General Don José Lopez Uraga, who not long ago was Mexican minister at Berlin. I beg Mr. Folsom, who was formerly the envoy from the United States to the Netherlands, to speak for the diplomatists.

Mr. FOLSOM.

Sir—Being at this moment invited to speak, it will be difficult for me to say any thing worthy of my hearers. Nevertheless, although without notice, I can not do less than accede to the request of our president. I have always been attached to the beautiful Castilian language—to that language so robust and manly, yet so soft and insinuating, which is capable of the highest flights of eloquence, as well as of the sweetest sentiments of love. Its study has occupied a part of my life, and I declare that it would have been difficult for me to have found a more delightful task. This love of the Spanish language could not but extend to the generous people who speak it, and more especially to the people of Spanish America, among whom Mexico occupies the first place, for its extent, resources, the beauty of its climate, the fertility of the soil, and, above all, from the very essential circumstance of being our neighbor, and having, since her emancipation, adopted republican institutions similar to those which have made our happiness. Guided by these sentiments, I undertook years ago a translation of the letters which Hernan Cortez addressed to the Emperor Charles the Fifth, giving an account of the conquest of New Spain—letters which contain very important historical data, and which were then entirely unknown to us until Mr. Prescott, our immortal historian, published his history of the conquest of Mexico. I say all this that it may be seen that my sympathy for the affairs of

Mexico is of long standing. And is it possible that it could cease to exist now that her sons are gloriously fighting to preserve an independence which it cost them so many sacrifices to achieve! No; certainly no. It exists in me now more actively than ever, as it does in the heart of every true American; for on this point, as some of the gentlemen have already well said, the opinion of our people is unanimous. Every one knows that on the Mexican soil a struggle is going on for a principle left us as an inheritance by one of our great statesmen, without adherence to which our institutions run great danger. I wish, then, that Mexico may sustain the struggle to which she has been so unjustly provoked, and I do not fear that I deceive myself in saying, in the name of the American people, that, as soon as our civil war is ended, our aid to Mexico will not be limited to barren sympathy.

THE CHAIR.

I have the pleasure to present to you Dr. NAVARRO, formerly chief of the medical staff of the Mexican army, during the defense of the city of Puebla. At the end of the siege, he delivered to the French surgeons the wounded prisoners, who had suffered amputation, in a convalescent state.

Will Dr. PARKER welcome Surgeon-General NAVARRO?

DR. PARKER.

MR. PRESIDENT AND GENTLEMEN—Dr. Navarro, whose health has been proposed, is the friend of man, whom we Americans delight to honor. We welcome him among us this evening as our guest.

It is true, sir, he has made himself eminent by his science and skill as a surgeon, and on that account he is entitled to our respect. But, Mr. President, it is not on account of his professional attainments that we seek to honor him this evening. It is because he has a loyal heart which beats in sympathy with our own, and, in these days, when treason is rampant, we feel ourselves attracted to every man whose bosom is warmed by the fire of true patriotism.

32

You have referred to Dr. Navarro's skill and humanity, always the unmistakable evidence of head and heart. Permit me here, sir, to state, that when the French authorities were made acquainted with the doctor's position and the happy results of his labors, every effort was made to induce him to turn traitor to his own Government. Honors and emoluments were proffered him, to be limited only by his own wishes. But he indignantly spurned them all.

So Hippocrates, the father of his profession, when Artaxerxes sought to attach him to his own court, striving by bribes and force to induce him to forsake Athens, exclaimed : " My talents, my art, my existence, all belong to Greece, and never can they be employed against my country."

Such, Mr. President, is Dr. Navarro, and we honor him and his compatriots—they have our sympathy. And, being in the right, it is my conviction and my faith, that the patriots of our sister republic must and will succeed.

" Magna est justitia et prævalebit."

THE CHAIR.

Dr. NAVARRO will, I am sure, do us the honor of speaking in reply.

DR. NAVARRO.

GENTLEMEN—I regret very much that my slight knowledge of your beautiful language does not permit me to duly express my feelings. I feel the greatest satisfaction in being a witness to the ardent sympathy manifested toward my dear country by persons of such a high social position and so respected for their scientific and literary knowledge. I have no words to express my gratitude for the toast and for the kind allusions which you have been pleased to make concerning me. Mexico, in defending her independence, has been struggling for a long time past with one of the most powerful monarchs of Europe, and she will struggle year after year, proving in this way the patriotic sentiments of her sons, and that she is worthy of that sympathy which all over the world every friend of justice and right shares with you in extending toward her. Please to receive, gentlemen, my most sincere prayers for the ending of your civil war—of the bloody struggle which has shaken this great Republic and given to European tyrants the opportunity of audaciously treading on the American continent—this sacred ground on which liberty only reigns, and in which thrones are but the sorrowful remembrances of times which will never return again. The time will come, and perhaps it is not very far off, when we shall see our republic free of all foreign intervention and your glorious Union happily restored—being once more, as it always has been, the astonishment of the civilized world and the fear of the despots of the Old World. (Cheers.)

THE CHAIR.

I beg leave to present to you Señor FERNANDO DE LA CUESTA, a member of the Mexican Legation. Himself a merchant, the commerce of New York should bid him welcome. In the hands of our late mayor, Mr. OPDYKE, also a merchant, the duties of hospitality will be best performed.

MR. OPDYKE.

MR. PRESIDENT AND GENTLEMEN—On behalf of the merchants of this city, and, I will venture to add, of the city itself, although it is no longer my privilege to speak officially in its name, I have great satisfaction in expressing profound sympathy for the cause which the people of our sister republic are sustaining against European invasion. I indorse fully and heartily all the sentiments uttered on this occasion by the enlightened and watchful friend of civil liberty on my left (W. C. Bryant, Esq.), his indignant protest against the attempt of Louis Napoleon to overthrow the Mexican republic, and to rear in its stead a despotism under the imperial sway of a Hapsburg, will, I am sure, meet an approving response from every true American.

The remarks of M. Thiers in the Corps Législatif of France, on the manner in which he believed the Archduke Maximilian would be received in this city, which our distinguished guest has referred to this evening, had not escaped my attention. Had the archduke ventured to test the sentiments of our people, I feel warranted in saying, that the distinguished French statesman would have found his expectations sadly disappointed.

The citizens of New York are not incapable of distinguishing between the friends and enemies of their country, and it is only to the former that they are in the habit of manifesting their respect and sympathy.

When the Russian fleet arrived in this port, I felt it to be my duty, as chief magistrate of the city, to invite the Common Council to extend to the Russian officers a prompt and generous hospitality. In making that recommendation, I correctly interpreted, as the result proved, the undivided sentiment of our people; for you all remember how the municipal authorities and the citizens vied with each other in extending a heartfelt welcome to the naval representatives of a great empire, which gave us, in our country's darkest hour of trial, unmistakable and touching evidence of its sympathy and friendship.

When, a little later, French and British vessels of war arrived at our port, it was suggested by a few that similar hospitalities should be extended to their officers. But I declined making the recommendation, on the ground that the Governments they represented had manifested toward our country, in its greatest need, sentiments directly opposite to those manifested by the Government and people of Russia; and in thus refusing I but conformed to the well-known sentiments and wishes of the great mass of our citizens.

So as regards the Archduke Maximilian, if he had touched at New York on his way to Mexico, a similar suggestion in his behalf would have been still more emphatically declined, because he was the instrument chosen by Louis Napoleon to consummate a high national crime against a neighboring republic as well as an act of marked unfriendliness to ourselves.

In a word, there is no difference of sentiment among our people on this subject. The universal feeling is earnestly hostile to any armed intervention of Europe on this continent, and especially to that which seeks to overthrow a republic in order to erect a monarchy.

SEÑOR DE LA CUESTA.

GENTLEMEN—It would be superfluous, perhaps presumptuous in me, to add one more word to what has been already said; yet I can not help tendering you my most sincere and heartfelt thanks for the beautiful manner in which you have been pleased to express your good wishes and warm sympathy for the land where I first saw the light and breathed the sweet air of life. As the last draught of water to the camel in the desert cheers and comforts him through the dreary path that lies before him, so will the remembrance of this night cheer and comfort me, whatever may be my path in life, to sustain the liberty, independence, and integrity of our national soil. I can not answer better the allusion, made by the gentleman who so worthily occupies the chair, as to my representing the commerce of Mexico, having once followed its pursuits, than by proposing the following toast:

The City of New York—first in sciences, arts, commerce, wealth; in fact, in all. First, also, let me add, in extending to us her noble sympathies for our holy cause. May she always prosper as she has hitherto prospered; and may she not only be the metropolis of the United States, but the metropolis of the whole world. (Cheers.)

THE CHAIR.

Mexico is not ignorant of the fine arts. The San Carlos Academy has produced painters and sculptors of distinguished merit. Among painters they have Cabrera, Cordero, Mata. Tolsa, an eminent architect, is known in Mexico by his beautiful Mining College. Will Mr. Sturges speak for the fine arts?

Mr. STURGES.

Mr. CHAIRMAN—I am taken quite by surprise in being called upon by you to respond to your allusion to the fine arts and architecture of Mexico. On some other occasion I should be most happy to speak upon such a theme; at present I prefer to speak a few words of encouragement to our distinguished guest, in the hope that his noble country may soon be free from her foreign and domestic enemies. When that is accomplished, we shall see every thing that is beautiful, noble, and useful springing to life with new vigor, and that glorious country will become all that God intended she should be. We know what it is, sir, to have foreign and domestic enemies, although we have no foreign enemy on our soil. It is not from any love which the enemy of Mexico bears us that his armies are not in Texas and Louisiana. It is the fear of his own people that restrains him. I have the word of a French gentleman, "who knows whereof he speaks," to support this statement. He said to me, "Rest assured, sir, the emperor will withdraw from Mexico the moment he can do so with any kind of credit to himself. The French people are against him in his Mexican movement, as they are against any interference in your affairs." I do not think, sir, that our honored guest can have failed to discover that the determination is as firmly fixed in the hearts of our people that no foreign government shall be established in Mexico, as it is that no separation shall take place between the States of this Union. Our own affairs settled, and it would not be sixty days before our armies would be in Mexico if her people desired it. My prayer to God is that she may hold out until we are ready for this. I respond most fully to the closing sentiment of my honorable friend, Mr. Bancroft: "Let the Austrian lamp burn in the grave of Austria; it will not burn in the free atmosphere of America." (Cheers.)

The CHAIR.

Mexico has had illustrious Governors. President Juarez was once Governor of the State of Oaxaca, and during the eight years of his administration he placed his State at the head of the Mexican Confederation. General Doblado has done the like for the State of Guanajuato. I give, then, honor to the Governors of the Mexican States. May we hope to hear from one of our company who has himself been Governor of New York, in reply?

Mr. WASHINGTON HUNT.

There being no correct report of Governor Hunt's speech, the following letter was received from him in reply to a request for a sketch of his remarks:

ALBEMARLE HOTEL, NEW YORK, March 31, 1864.

DEAR SIR—It would afford me pleasure to comply with the request contained in your note of yesterday, but as my remarks were desultory and unprepared, instead of attempting an accurate sketch, I will confine myself to two leading points, which I deem of the most essential import at the present juncture.

1. I intended to utter an earnest and emphatic protest against the French invasion of Mexico, and the audacious efforts to overthrow the republic and to erect upon its ruins a monarchy, to be upheld by a foreign force, acting in conjunction with a small faction of domestic traitors. I denounced it as a wanton offense against republican liberty and the independence of nations.

2. I intended to express the opinion that the United States will not permit, for any long period, the armed occupation of Mexico by a foreign power.

Our domestic conflict will terminate in the re-establishment of the national authority over all the States of the Union. The attainment of this result is not, I trust, very far distant.

Then the people of this country will manifest their sympathy for the people of Mexico in active and efficient co-operation; and, if need be, they will rally to your aid in a resolute and manly struggle for the recovery of your national liberty and independence.

F

The time approaches when our Government will reassert and maintain its well-defined policy, which is, that no European power shall be allowed to subjugate the people or destroy republican institutions on any part of the American continent.

I remain, with great respect,

Your obedient servant,

WASHINGTON HUNT.

Hon. MATIAS ROMERO, &c., &c., &c.

THE CHAIR.

There are historians, too, in Mexico—Mora, Tavala, and Bustamente are not unknown names in literature. Will the President of the New York Historical Society respond?

MR. DE PEYSTER.

I yield, sir, to your request, merely in the private character in which I appear here this evening. I came to express, by my presence, the sympathy which I feel toward a sister republic, torn by intestine strife, brought upon her by a party that should have soothed, not inflicted, a national wound. I am reminded of the sad position of Mexico by the like sad realities which press upon my country. I know full well what would be the intensity of my feelings were my native land invaded by foreign bayonets, to compel her to change her free Government for one obnoxious to her people. I came here with a further view—to testify toward our distinguished guest my respect and admiration of his patriotic devotion to the country which he so ably represents, and my deep interest in the cause which he so nobly sustains—not by words—for I came, not to speak, but to be an attentive listener, and therefore took no thought with reference to such a request.

But, Mr. Chairman, being up, I have ideas furnished by the suggestive remarks just made by Señor Romero. I well remember the *points* presented by him in December last, in a speech made on an occasion similar to the present. He considered the Church party in Mexico as the direct cause of the civil war there, as slavery is of the rebellion here. He alleged that this Church party sought foreign intervention to re-establish its power there, as the slave power here sought the like intervention, in order to build up a confederacy based on the perpetual sacrifice of certain human rights, and designed to be antagonistic to our national sovereignty.

Thus far this parallel between the United States and Mexico truly extends, in regard to the present condition of each. But, sir, there is a difference in the analogy of these cases not to be overlooked. Were foreign intervention to take here the course it has pursued in Mexico, the result in this country would be as a tornado is to the storm now sweeping over our land. England and France know this! It is not their good-will that stays their further interference, but the danger of the risk from the blows which a free people, aroused to do their utmost at any sacrifice, could and would inflict in return.

Educated in the school of democracy, I have, sir, adhered to the principles learned there. When our civil war broke out, I had doubts, on constitutional grounds, regarding the rights of slave-owners. But when I observed how slaves were made instruments to defeat freemen striving to preserve the Union, in a military point of view I considered that it was indispensable to strike from the hands of rebels their main prop; and all my constitutional scruples vanished before this military necessity. I believe, sir, all loyal men—loyal without mental reservations—deem it right to remove any obstacle for the preservation of the Union! Therefore, I have no affinity with traitors, either South or in disguise among us, who keep "the promise to the ear;" or with "peace Democrats," in my judgment more alive to party interest than to our national struggle.

What, sir, is the result thus far in *our* civil war? Why, as slavery proved itself to have been the source of all our evils, loyal men gave it its death-blow. Like all monsters of great strength, determined purpose, and defiant resistance, it will die hard: but, despite its struggles, die it must and will!

Now, from our conflict let me for a few moments turn to our sister republic and to her accumulated ills, and contrast her purposes with our own. Mexico, with a fertile soil, genial climate, and unbounded mineral wealth, is divided into various conflicting parties. Her Church party is the predominant class, intent upon maintaining its present influence and recovering its lost power; there are also the patriots, struggling for the Government of their choice; and, if I am rightly informed, there is another class, influenced by the ecclesiastics, either hostile to or indifferent toward the present republican form of government.

It is said that the Church party now wavers in its appreciation of French intervention. If this be so, and Mexicans would unitedly and heroically rally as the people of our loyal States have rallied, the ills which Mexico is now experiencing would be in the condition of the monster evil that we have mortally wounded. The form of domestic treason in Mexico we know. The motives of the French Emperor are too patent to be disguised. Señor Romero has thrown ample light on both these subjects.

Whether a recently-published mention of a leave-taking between the Emperor and his Austrian *protégé* be true, or a *jeu d'esprit*, it is suggestive of probable ground of belief. "You go," said the former, "to embrace a rock of silver"—a figure of speech which symbolized the mineral wealth, of which Mexican bars of silver and Mexican dollars had proved to be in Europe the best of advertisements.

The Church party in Mexico had long suffered under a disease of very great prevalence at all times and everywhere in Europe, where its influence is all powerful. The Emperor caught it through this party contact, and he gave it to his Austrian favorite. This disease in ancient Rome was called "*auri sacra fames*" There, where the central word (*sacra*) was connected with offerings to the infernal deities, or with impious or unholy purposes, it meant the reverse of its proper definition, namely, *accursed*. The tripartite association just alluded to, under the hallucination created by this disease, have this "accursed desire of wealth;" and think to overthrow the Mexican republic, to build up in its stead a monarchy, by the instrumentality of French bayonets, and thus possess this " rock of silver."

Sir, the snake is the emblem of evil! We took the reptile up when feeble, and warmed it in the national bosom. When it gained strength, it turned and stung us. It has its reward! If Mexicans will rally round their national standard, and imitate the gallant bird on their national arms, who has in his beak a malignant snake, and, with his determined courage and undaunted decision, extinguish, like him, the reptile's ability to do further mischief, all will yet go well in their beautiful land. In due season, our rebels will be compelled to "succumb" to the loyal will. Then the republics of North America will shake hands in brotherly sentiment and alliance, and unitedly maintain inviolate the Monroe doctrine.

This doctrine, sir, is destined to become dominant on this Continent. It has a definite object in view, to be carried out peaceably if it can, but forcibly if it must be so! That object, it appears to me, may be summed up in a few words, as in the case before us. France, guided by a *Napoleonic idea*, taking advantage of a civil war of unparalleled magnitude in the American republic, thinks the occasion an opportune one to establish a dynastic form of government on our borders, which is congenial with European systems but antagonistic to democratic institutions. Her imperial ruler uses, for his purposes, a scion of the house of Hapsburg, to build up, on the ruins of the Mexican republic, an empire which is to strengthen and extend the power and influence of the Latin races ; and by this course of propagandism to establish on this vast continent dynasties, also, congenial with the views and prejudices of the ruling classes in Europe. This is in direct conflict with the principles and rights recognized by, and dear to, the American people.

Such an experiment would never have been made, but for the civil war now raging in the United States. Under no circumstances will the American Republic permit foreign interference of this kind with her republican institutions, or for the overthrow, by foreign bayonets, of similar systems in North America, in order to introduce in their stead a form of government hateful to those to whom the principle of freedom is dear, and independence a reality!

In the hearts of Frenchmen smolders the fire of *Liberty, Fraternity,* and *Equality.* A war against freedom in America—which belongs to the people—could not fail, in France, to rekindle that fire. Intelligent Frenchmen know that the great Julius aimed to control the destinies of a world; and in his fate anticipate that of his proclaimed imitator.

Is France, in Mexico, fighting "for an idea"? Who doubts it? It is the idea of remuneration. The United States are also now actually fighting at home for an idea, but it is the *idea of freedom.* France, under her present dynasty, can have no sympathy with the AMERICAN IDEA; for that tends to democracy.

History is constantly repeating itself. Should the torch in "revolutionary" France be relighted, Frenchmen could read by its blaze a "writing" far older than France itself: "Thou art weighed in the balance, and art found wanting."

The Monroe doctrine has, with this exposition, also this teaching—that a mighty nation is marching on to guard its destined course. (Applause.)

The CHAIR.

Brooklyn, our neighbor, desires to do honor also to our guests. Will Mr. Henry E. Pierrepont, one of her honored sons, tell us what Brooklyn thinks of Maximilian?

Mr. PIERREPONT.

Mr. HENRY E. PIERREPONT then spoke, and in short and eloquent phrases said that he was sure that the feelings of the citizens of Brooklyn, with respect to the French policy in Mexico, were identical with those of the citizens of New York and of the entire country; that on that account, and fearing to tire the audience, he would not speak at length on the subject.

The CHAIR.

The Bar of New York will not consent to withhold its own words of cheer. Will Mr. Clift *say* what the lawyers *say* about Mexico?

Mr. CLIFT.

Mr. President and Gentlemen—Considering the lateness of the hour, and my own indisposition, my remarks must necessarily be few, but to remain on an occasion like this entirely silent I can not.

Descended from ancestors who fought for the liberties and independence of my own country, I should belie every instinct of my nature and every tradition of my race, were I to withhold an expression of sympathy and encouragement to any nation struggling to be free; and much more, to withhold it from our friends and neighbors, the people of Mexico, in this their hour of need.

I belong, sir, to the legal profession, whose members, in all ages and in all countries, have ever been foremost, not only as the advocates of liberty and justice, but the leaders in all political reforms and revolutions; and I think I hazard nothing in saying that if the sentiments of the members of the Bar of this city, to which I have the honor to belong, could be known this night, they would be found universally in favor of republican government everywhere on this continent, and in perfect harmony with what has been said here this evening on that subject.

The great public opinion of this country is also in harmony with this same sentiment; and if there is any deeply-settled conviction in the loyal American mind and heart upon any subject whatsoever, more than upon any other, it is, first, that the fearful rebellion now raging in our midst shall be put down; and, second, that republican institutions alone shall prevail from the Atlantic to the Pacific and from the St. Lawrence to the Isthmus of Darien.

With no desire to longer trespass upon your patience, and with the most hearty good-will for our guest of this evening, and the people and cause he represents, permit me to give you the Mexican war-cry—"*God and Liberty.*"

THE CHAIR.

The literary men have not all spoken. Let us hear from Mr. Bristed.

MR. CHARLES ASTOR BRISTED.

Once upon a time the Saracens—then a mighty people—took it into their heads that it would be a nice thing to conquer Old Spain, and they did conquer Spain so effectually that it took eight hundred years to drive them out. But they were driven out, and none of them are there at this day. I believe that, in like manner, the French will be driven out of Mexico, if it takes eight hundred years to do so.

(A gentleman exclaimed, "We do things faster now-a-days. Say eight years.")

THE CHAIR.

Shall we not hear also from our young and distinguished friend,— who may worthily assume to speak for Young America—Mr. Dodge.

MR. WILLIAM E. DODGE, JR.

As perhaps the youngest, Mr. Chairman, who has been honored by an invitation on this most interesting and delightful occasion, it is my right and privilege to speak for the young men of our country, and I can assure our honored guest that their full and entire sympathy is with him and with his oppressed country.

The tread of a French invasion is to them a direct insult, and, were our own sad war over, I believe there is not a town, or village, or hamlet, where a full company would not spring to arms, to aid our sister republic in her glorious struggle.

I give, sir, as a sentiment, in which I know all will heartily join—

The Monroe Doctrine—Americans can never allow the heel of European despotism to place its imprint upon the soil of our Western Continent.

The CHAIR.

Gentlemen—Let us now recognize the services of our commissariat, who have so nobly discharged their stewardship. I propose—

The health of the Stewards.

I beg Mr. Hamersley to speak in their behalf. (Three cheers were given for the Committee.)

Mr. JOHN W. HAMERSLEY.

It is hardly fair, sir, to call on us while your hearts are beating with fervid thoughts, and your ears ringing with burning words. Had this toast been on the programme, one of my coadjutors would have prepared an address worthy of the compliment and the occasion. This Committee was not chosen for their gifts of utterance, but for those humbler tastes, which only lend a grace to eloquence. Our duties are æsthetic, industrial, and artistic. We have compassed the ends of the earth, the depths of the sea; we have levied contributions on the four winds of heaven, to cluster here all that can tempt the appetite, or fascinate the ear and eye, and we fancied our mission accomplished.

However, there is the post-prandial law; the despotism of the wine cup, to which we all owe allegiance—the only despotism, which the descendants of the Huguenots, or Pilgrim Fathers, will ever tolerate on this Continent. We are here, sir, in menace to none, but firmly and respectfully in the majesty of manhood, and in consciousness of power, to reassert a principle, imbibed with our mothers' milk, a household word, a dogma of American faith; but while we cordially grasp our neighbor's hand, in the darkest hour of her trial, that grasp has due emphasis and significance.

With her, we have kindred traditions: each of us has hewn an empire from the wilderness; each of us has expelled the oppressor;

c

and both of us, with tattered banners drenched in the gore of hero martyrs, are now appealing from treachery to the God of Battles.

We have a common future; for who can doubt that our successes (and the death-knell of treason has already rung)—who can doubt that the triumph of our arms, will be the signal for the eagles of Austerlitz, "to change their base," from the pyramids of Puebla, for their perch on the towers of Notre Dame? And permit me here, sir, to express a hope, suggested by the *season*, (God grant it may be a prophecy,) that the Easter chimes of Mexico, of the coming year, with the glad tidings of a Saviour risen, shall peal from sierra to sierra, from ocean to ocean, with the glad tidings of a nation risen, a nation born again. (Cheers.)

Mr. Chairman, I would offer a toast seldom forgotten in this Eden of women. It is wise, to fling the garland of chivalry over the stern realities of life, nay, over the carnage of the battle-field. It is graceful in our honored guests, to seek in the bright eyes, and warm hearts of those they love, in their sunset home, a solace for hope deferred. It is meet in us all, revelling amid these symbols of hope, and joy, of passion and power, our twin standards, nestling in each other's folds in sweet communion of the storied past, and soaring hope, (these roses and violets, breathing incense to the throne of grace, their Easter hymn of thanks, and praise,) to remember, who it is that scatters these jewels of Paradise over our thorny path, who it is that smooths the pillow of affliction.

And when our statesman soldier [to Romero] shall send these our greetings to his fatherland, let him say, that these are sons of sires, who wielded the destinies of our country, whose names, are carved on her escutcheon, like the name of Phidias on the shield of Minerva. Here, are her merchant princes, whose argosies girdle the globe; here, are her gifted men, whose thoughts touch the hearts or nerve the souls of the nomad in his desert, and the prince upon his throne. Say, sir, that here is our western lark, who lends to devotion the muses' wings. Say, that the author of "Thanatopsis," and these sons, worthy of their sires, send a brother's blessing to sisters bowed in grief. Fire their souls with the thrilling words of the Spartan matron, giving a shield to her son :—

" Return with this or upon this."

Tell them, of the mother of the Gracchi, whose only jewels were her sons; tell them, of the death-dirge of our red man, with " back to the field and feet to the foe ;" tell them, that the spirit of your own Guatimozin hovers over your war-path, and exhort, nay, adjure them to swear their brothers, over the fresh graves of their comrades, never to bury the tomahawk, while the iron heel of Europe treads your soil.

Sir [to the Chair], it is fitting, while the accents of sweet music recall tender, and happy memories (man, imaged by that armed cactus ; woman, by that graceful palm), it is holy, to consecrate the hour to her, who was "last at the cross and first at the sepulchre." I propose, sir, a toast, to which your heart's pulse will echo :

The daughters of Mexico—Fair as her sons are brave.

(Enthusiastic and prolonged applause. Music— *Viva Republica.*)

The Chair.

We must not permit the modesty of our banker and steward, Mr. Clews, to outweigh our desire to hear from the Bourse.

Mr. Henry Clews.

Mr. President and Gentlemen—Enough has already been said, in the speeches made this evening, to indicate most conclusively the depth of sympathy which pervades this community in behalf of the cause of Mexico, and I rise to express my cordial concurrence with the sentiments which have been avowed.

The unanimous and determined voices of this company clearly show, that public opinion in this country will not submit to the encroachments of foreign powers upon any portion of the territory of this Continent.

The principles of free republican government are so strongly implanted in the hearts of the people, both of Mexico and the United States, that they will never consent to surrender them.

Human freedom, and the rights of man make common cause between Mexico and all other American States.

I do not utter these words in prejudice against any government. In my judgment, European nations will best promote the welfare of their own people by carefully abstaining from all interference with the declared will of those who dwell on this Continent.

The doctrine has been solemnly asserted, and will be maintained inviolate against all alliances which seek to impede the progress of liberal institutions, or to impair the strength of governments founded on the rights and intelligence of the people.

This is the doctrine of the United States, and, under the shield of its power and influence, the safety, prosperity, and independence of Mexico will be maintained and made perpetual. (Cheers.)

It was after midnight, and the fervor of that earnest group had not abated ; and who will wonder, that, surrounded by the traditions of home ; her sweet music, her defiant armorial bearings ; her forest foliage ; her flag so often dyed with his blood ; while cheers loud, and long, for his gallant country, rang through those brilliant halls, mingling with the "Buenas noches" of the band, as each grasped his hands, and bid him, "God speed," that emotion was betrayed, in the quivering lip, and moistened eye of Romero.

It may be a grave consideration for foreign usurpers, that, a few days subsequently, the House of Representatives "unanimously" resolved, that the United States would never consent to the establishment of a monarchy which would arise under the auspices of Europe, upon the ruins of a republic on the American Continent.

A prince of Hapsburg, whose family boast the blood of the Roman Cæsar—their record, the history of oppression—is called by the one, free, and cordial voice of Mexico, to occupy her "silver throne."

Look on that picture, now look on this:—

With forty thousand foreign bayonets, missionaries from the "Empire of Peace" to his loyal subjects; his treasury bankrupt; French guerrillas, prowling about the gates of his capital; his waking spectre, the assassin's dagger; his dream, the vengeance of desolated homes—like a true disciple of Machiavel, he rivets on the free American, the shackles we have just struck from the African: and, in the same decree, lauds the devotion of the noble JUAREZ, and in the name of humanity, dooms him to a felon's death. Verily! the tool of Napoleon, on his "silver throne," wears a crown of thorns.

MR. SEWARD TO MR. ROMERO.

DEPARTMENT OF STATE,
WASHINGTON, June 2, 1864.

SIR—I have the honor to acknowledge the receipt of your note of the 28th ultimo, covering a translation into the English language of the documents previously inclosed to me in your unofficial note of the 26th ultimo.

I avail, &c.,

WILLIAM H. SEWARD.

Señor M. ROMERO, &c., &c., &c.